AF595498

JOB SEARCH AFTER JOB LOSS

NEIL O'DONNELL

Copyright (C) 2021 Neil O'Donnell

Layout design and Copyright (C) 2021 by Next Chapter

Published 2021 by Next Chapter

Edited by Brice Fallon

Cover art by CoverMint

Back cover texture by David M. Schrader, used under license
from Shutterstock.com

All rights reserved. No part of this book may be reproduced or transmitted in any form or by any means, electronic or mechanical, including photocopying, recording, or by any information storage and retrieval system, without the author's permission.

CONTENTS

I dedicate this book to my network of family and friends, all of whom supported and guided me after I was laid off the week before my wedding. It was a scary and chaotic time, and you all were a great support.

INTRODUCTION

Losing a job is an extremely painful experience. If you are reading this, you likely understand this all too well, especially given the loss of jobs due to the COVID Pandemic. When I was laid off, I could barely eat or sleep in the days that immediately followed. Because it was the week before my wedding, I think you can imagine I was beyond anxious, starting a family with no job. Job loss shows us just how integral to our personal identity a job is. Without the job, we tend to lose focus in our daily lives; a reality that leads to struggles in multiple areas of life: relationships, hobbies, and relaxation. Consequently, it is critical for individuals to immediately embrace their job search and make every effort to seek employment opportunities daily. Don't know where to start a job search or how to create job application materials (résumés, CVs, or cover letter)? No worries — that's what I am here for.

About Me

So, what the hell do I know about job searches, résumés, and career counseling? I'm glad you asked! I am a nationally-certified, professional career coach (CPCC) and professional member of the Professional Association of Résumé Writers & Career Coaches. My certification was attained after hours (and hours) of study and successfully completing testing on résumé writing (and submitting sample résumés), interviewing skills, and career counseling.

My actual career-counseling experience spans two decades and includes helping recent graduates and recently fired/laid off professionals who were not far away from retiring. I myself was laid off from a job the week before my wedding, so I know all too well the pressure of losing a job. It is a gut-wrenching situation that pummels an individual with stress, fear, and feelings of inadequacy. Since my own battle with unemployment, I have successfully worked to help hundreds find jobs. This includes providing career counseling for sales associates, engineers, computer programmers, psychologists, social workers, chemists, chefs, waiters, librarians, authors, biologists, event planners, teachers, criminologists, artists, nutritionists, business managers, editors, journalists, marketing & PR specialists, and accountants. For the record, the strategies I use with clients to find a good job are the very strategies I used after getting laid off. The results of those strategies for me? With degrees in Anthropology and living in a city whose economy had been struggling for decades, I found a better-paying (Anthropology-related) job in two months, which was within walking distance of my home.

Why Write This Book?

Getting fired or laid off is truly traumatic, because those in such situations usually aren't expecting it. Then, in the immediate aftermath, a fired/laid off individual endures an emotional journey with thoughts of never finding another job or questions of what the individual did that caused the job loss. From my experience, it is often months before a fired or laid off worker is emotionally ready to truly focus on a job search. That is why I wrote this book. Waiting to invest quality time into a job search hurts, because any delay leads to more stress, a loss of job opportunities, and a loss of potential earnings (immediate earnings, health benefits, AND retirement savings)! The wait also can take its toll on a job seeker's health and wellness, which alone is reason enough to invest quality time and effort into searching for work immediately.

1

I'VE LOST MY JOB! NOW WHAT?

Let's pull the Band-Aid off! You lost your job! Regardless of the reason for the job loss, it is usually unexpected and almost always heart wrenching. For what you are enduring and for what you will endure, I am extremely sorry. For those who were laid off due to budget cuts/loss of grant funding, I know that this feels like someone pulled the rug out from under you. I know at least that is how I felt when it happened to me. For those fired for a job mishap, no words I say will likely soften the blow. Justified or not, getting fired is painful! By the way, we all mess up at work; no one is perfect!

Whatever the cause of a job loss, it is a painful experience that causes us to feel alone, helpless, defeated, ashamed, and/or without hope. Well, I'm here to tell you that that is all the time we have to dwell on the job loss. Do you feel better? No, the sting from a job loss stays with you for quite some time. However, it is imperative that you don't dwell on the event itself. Why? First of all, your health and general wellbeing is at risk if you don't put things into perspective. As a career counselor and stress management coach, I can tell you that individuals that dwell on the job loss event generally lose a lot of sleep and fail to eat properly. That loss of sleep and nutrition causes many individuals to ultimately need medical attention, which costs money a newly unemployed person needs for rent or food. Do you see the trap? Likewise, as an individual who has battled an anxiety disorder for his whole life, dwelling on such a traumatic event can lead to long-term health issues, which won't become evident until years later. For these reasons alone, it is imperative that you accept the event and move on.

Still dwelling on the event? Consider this.

Every day spent dwelling on the event of losing your job is a day spent away from getting out and searching for a new job, which delays actually obtaining a new job. The result of this means a loss of lifetime earnings, a reduction in funds built up for retirement, and a delay in gaining the satisfaction a job often brings to a person. Think about it: our jobs, even on bad days, often provide us direction and the satisfaction that we have worked towards some goal. Yes, many people find things outside of employment that give them satisfaction. However, we generally have much of our pride tied to our jobs. Dwelling on a job loss delays our getting back to having such a driving force in our lives. For these reasons, it is imperative that you put the job loss event behind you. Learn from the experience and move on.

Getting Support: Your Network and Physician

As I previously remarked, I was laid off unexpectedly AND I have battled an anxiety disorder my whole life. Needless to say, I was put in a tough position of having a difficult time letting go and not dwelling on the job loss event. Whether you have an overriding health concern or not, you too may find it difficult to put aside the job loss event on your own. In such circumstances, I implore you to seek help. First, look to colleagues and friends, your network, for encouragement during this time. Yes, I understand it's embarrassing to tell people you lost your job. However, your network of colleagues and friends can help you boost your ego and alleviate your stress, which is critical to your physical and mental health. As for your primary care physician, he/she can help alleviate your stress as well, whether it's through consultation or medication. In my case, given my anxiety, my physician prescribed an antidepressant in addition to referring me to a psychologist to help address the job-loss stress. I am forever grateful for what my doctor did for me, and many will likewise benefit from medical assistance. Talk to your doctor immediately after a job loss to determine what assistance you may need.

Another source of support is likely available to you: staff from the college or high school you graduated from. Professional staff and faculty from career centers, college counseling centers, alumni affairs offices, and major departments often provide guidance to unemployed graduates. Whether it's connecting you with another alum working in a similar field or it's a staff member specialized in career searches, the support you receive (often free of charge) could provide the personal support you need to start an effective career search AND manage the stress and anxiety that come with having lost a job.

Unjustified Firing

In the event you feel your firing or lay off was unjustified, I recommend you seek guidance from an attorney specialized in labor issues. An attorney can provide you with a better understanding of what options you have for filing a claim as well as what long-term effects any litigation will have. Remember to ask an attorney what her/his fees are before signing anything (including what an initial consultation costs).

Before a Job Search: Getting Set

Are you ready? Seriously, are you ready? Before venturing forward in search of a good job, there is a list of things you need to take care of, preparations you must make. It's not just from the financial side of things either. To effectively search for a job, you need a team behind you. Are you worried about hiring someone to help with your job search? If you can afford to hire someone to help, great! Yet, that's not the team I am referring to. Here is a preparation list for anyone looking for a new job, which includes strategies specifically for someone who was fired or laid off from a job.

- ***Enlist the aid of your network***: I've said it before and I'll say it again: your network of family, friends, and colleagues are a crucial outlet for finding jobs. It is especially important to reach out to colleagues and references from previous jobs to let them know you are unemployed and seeking a job. Be specific in letting your network know what you are looking for. They can relay that to their own networks, which will increase the number of people looking out for you. Also, with regards from your college professors, it is imperative that you reach out to the department from which you received your college degree. Between the department's staff and employees in your alma mater's Alumni Affairs Office, you should be able to connect with individuals best suited to finding a job opening best fitting your qualifications and career goals. Just so you know, businesses often call colleges for a list of recent graduates suited for job openings the companies have, because one phone call to a college could save a business thousands of dollars spent in job advertising and interviewing.

- ***Assess your necessary expenses and savings:*** Without your job, you will have limited or no money coming in. Consequently, it is imperative that you examine what money you have saved, what money (unemployment funds) you will have coming in, and what new expenses you will have to now manage in addition to the necessary expenses you will need to manage. The savings should be relatively easy to determine, but calculating what income you will still receive may take some time. First, take account of any remaining checks your now ex-employer will be sending you (remaining paychecks and any compensation for remaining vacation and sick time). Then, go to the unemployment office to complete paperwork so you can receive unemployment benefits. The unemployment office will likely require you to attend a workshop or seminar on job searching before they release funds. Consequently, you need to go to the unemployment office as soon as possible after losing a job to ensure that unemployment funds arrive immediately. Before the first check arrives, ask the office what amount of weekly/bi-weekly funds you will be receiving. Once you have your funds assessed, determine what bills are necessary and which are luxuries. Cut out any luxuries such as cable television, a landline phone (if you also have a cell phone), magazine subscriptions, and memberships to gyms or other organizations. You may also want to look into downsizing to a cheaper apartment and use of public transportation, the latter to cut down on car insurance and maintenance bills. As for living space, consider moving in with family if that is an option. Lastly, determine what health insurance options you have. This is something to discuss with your ex-employer, because you may be entitled to COBRA.

Regardless of health insurance options, you will likely have to spend more out of pocket for such insurance.

- ***Visit unemployment office:*** I already touched upon this in the last paragraph, but I just want to discuss the unemployment office again briefly. When at the unemployment office, make certain you ask them about how long your benefits will continue for. Additionally, ask what is required of you. They are likely going to require that you show proof that you are actively seeking employment while you receive benefits. Later I will discuss a chart I developed to record my job searches, a chart developed in part as documentation for the unemployment office (if you don't show effort in searching for a job, you could lose your unemployment benefits). Another thing of importance with regards to the unemployment office is that they have resources and job listings to help the unemployed find jobs. Their career counselors could likewise provide great guidance on alternate outlets for jobs (staff members at these offices often know of local businesses that are currently hiring). You can also inquire with unemployment office staff what health benefits may be available for you depending on COBRA payments as discussed in the last paragraph.
- ***Manage money:*** While this may go without saying, I want to stress the importance of managing your money during a job search. I'm not going to say you can never go out to lunch with a friend or that you can't go to a movie now and then. However, you need to be careful how you spend what money you have. Once you know what money is coming in (savings, unemployment benefits, etc.), budget those funds. Set aside money weekly for food, rent, and other necessities. Then, with what is remaining, try to save what you can while

leaving a little for luxury expenses. As for savings, you may need to purchase a new suit or pay for travel expenses when you start interviewing for jobs, which is why you definitely have to try to save money when possible.

- ***Freelancing:*** The Internet provides an unlimited number of opportunities for individuals to freelance in order to earn additional money; sites like Upwork.com and Fiverr.com are great resources in this regard. Likewise, you may be able to find part-time employment to help bring in a small amount of money to tide you over until you have a new full-time job. That said, make certain you discuss with the unemployment office what impact such jobs will have on your unemployment benefits AND discuss with the IRS your tax liabilities on such income.
- ***Avoid touching retirement savings:*** For those with retirement accounts, I strongly recommend that you think twice before pulling money from such accounts. Between the penalties for early withdraws of money to the loss in interest revenue long-term, it will likely be unwise to use these funds. If you have a family, you may have little choice, which I understand. I would recommend that you speak with an accountant BEFORE using such funds to determine how withdrawing these funds will impact you immediately and after retirement.
- ***Find time to relax every day:*** I know it sounds ludicrous to suggest that you find time to relax. After losing my job, I was beyond stressed to say the least. Given that, how can I seriously advise someone else who lost a job that he or she makes sure to relax every day. As I remarked earlier, stress can cause physical and mental health problems for individuals. For instance, an influx of stress could make someone irritable,

something that will strain relationships and possibly spill over in a job interview causing you to not get hired. Stress could lead to sickness, which may require doctor visits that ultimately deplete savings. For these reasons, I advise you to find time every single day to relax, whether it's taking time to watch a favorite television show, read a book, or go for a hike in the woods. For your physical and mental wellbeing, you need this time to relax and recharge.

Documenting Your Job Search

To maintain unemployment benefits, you will likely be required to show effort with regards to actively searching for work. To make things easier for yourself, I suggest creating a chart like the example below. During my own job search, I included columns for Job applied to, the company the job was with, the date I applied, the date of a response (and what the response was), and whether I sent a thank you note (I always encourage sending thank you notes because it's the right thing to do and it may get you considered for other positions). Other columns to include are date of interview, contact person, and notes.

Job	Company	Date applied	Response	Response Date	Thank You Sent
Career Advisor	Erie College	30-Jun	Interview date set for July 28	5-Jul	
Job Coach	Buffalo County	2-Jul			
PR Assistant	Ad Agency Inc.	5-Jul	Did not get job/interview	12-Jul	Yes

Now, with your chart set and information recorded, there are two other reasons I strongly encourage clients to record their job search efforts. First, from personal experience going through a job search after a job loss, I remember continually questioning whether or not I was doing everything I could to track down jobs. Years later, having helped hundreds of individuals with job searches, I find such concerns to be near universal. A chart like what I suggest can provide an instant affirmation that you are making strides. I still have my job search notes from 2003, the year I lost my job and then had to find new employment. I look at that chart and remember how I felt proud of my efforts, and that pride helped me get through low points.

As for the second reason, when you start looking at job postings day in and day out, things can become a blur. Maintaining a record of jobs you applied for can help ensure that you do not apply for a job twice. Such a mistake could make a job seeker appear unorganized. That is not a first impression you want to make to any prospective employer. Refer to this record every time you find a new job so you can verify if you applied for the job previously.

2

UPDATE RÉSUMÉ AND ONLINE PROFILES

A job seeker by default is a salesperson. As a salesperson, it is necessary to present your product (you) in the best light possible: as an accomplished professional that others enjoyed working with. Such "advertising" begins with your résumé and online profiles.

The Résumé Update

Let's face it: the résumé is on the front lines in the war to find employment. Whether in digital form (LinkedIn profile or as an email uploaded to a company's server) or as a traditional paper document mailed in or dropped off at an employer's office, the résumé is a critical component to helping job seekers get noticed. For those declaring that résumés will soon be irrelevant, think again. LinkedIn and other online outlets are years away from taking over, as are most hiring managers years away from accessing LinkedIn or personal websites to review a candidate's qualifications and work history. Simply look at the "jobs" section of your weekly newspaper. Many of jobs listed will likely include instructions to "email a résumé" for consideration. Yes, digital résumés are the new norm, but it's the traditional résumé format nonetheless.

So, how do you best advertise yourself when job searching? You make certain your résumé is updated with all relevant jobs and skill sets. Now, if you were fired from a job, you may want to consider whether or not to include that job on your résumé. If you had been at the job for multiple years and/or the job provided the necessary training and experience for a job you are applying to, then you will need to include it on your résumé. For jobs you had for a short time, it's easier to just leave it off your résumé to avoid having to explain a firing and any related issues. Now, as for résumé updates, there are some basic guidelines a job seeker should keep in mind.

- **Update contact information.** You'd be amazed at how often job seekers have an old cell phone number or email address listed on her/his résumé. Don't make this mistake.
- **Update your education and training.** Many job seekers complete continuing education credits every year. Listing such education could prove essential to landing a new job especially if a workshop you attended relates well to a job you are applying for. A final note, many employers like to see and hire applicants who continue to learn new industry procedures. **As for recently fired individuals, continuing education credits could help improve your image in the eyes of a hiring manager as individuals who seek continued training and knowledge often appear as hardworking and dependable.**
- **Identify career accomplishments on your résumé.** The next chapter provides guidance on the structure of a professional résumé. In the area reserved for

"professional and volunteer experience," it is critical that you identify things you accomplished at each job. What did you do that was above and beyond the call of duty? Did you develop a new training program? Did you exceed sales goals? Did you obtain grants to fund company operations or staff? Did you revamp the computer systems for a previous employer? Employers spend a lot of money on searching for new employees. Standard background checks alone could cost hundreds of dollars. To cut down on costs, employers are screening applicants for individuals who have demonstrated their ability to excel and bring drive and determination to the workplace. Accomplishments are what help employers identify such talent. Don't just list basic duties. Instead, list at least one accomplishment for each job posted on your résumé. For those early in their careers, make every effort to accomplish something noteworthy at every job you have. Here are a few examples of noteworthy accomplishments:

Led effort to expand company's customer base into new region, which led to a 25% increase in customers and 35% increase in revenue from services rendered.

Award-winning customer service representative with 100% quality assurance rating. Skilled at mediating customer complaints and queries.

Led initiative to transfer business records over to Excel-based database and archive providing staff a secure and global 24-hour access to customer & inventory files.

Created online archive of all past publications, which provided members with 24/7 access to all articles. Secured private grant to provide local high schools free access to archive.

Secured government grants in excess of $50,000 to fund after-school programs for youth in foster care.

Published journalist with articles appearing in Tech Magazine and Tech World Journal. Developed and edited Technology Column for 21st Century News Journal.

Instrumental in expanding 21st Century News Journal to digital media. Created and managed the 21st Century News Journal's Twitter, Facebook, Blab, and LinkedIn pages.

Implemented continuing education programming for staff in areas of sales practices, customer service operations, and finance industry technological developments.

Implemented continuing education program, which provided nursing staff with updated training in stress management, HIPPA regulations, and integrative health therapies.

Secured private grant to fund continuing education for institution's staff in areas of child development, classroom management, health & wellness, and first aid.

- Update technological proficiencies. I am over 40 years of age and still a tech specialist that even IT professionals seek assistance from. For a person without a cell phone or a computer science degree, that's quite unique, wouldn't you say? I hate phones (hence, the reason I have no cell phone), but I love technology in general. My technological background includes managing multiple blogs, creating web pages, developing & overseeing company Twitter pages, and even restoring data from old memory devices (most recently a 3.5" diskette). You see, I continually invest time learning new technologies so that I remain relevant, which is something companies love to see. You should make certain that you stay up to date on basic programs and indicate your computer proficiencies on your résumé. For the record, Microsoft Excel is still one of the go-to programs for many businesses and will likely remain so for the next 5 to 10 years…so learn it. Mastering PowerPoint, Access, creating web pages and utilizing accounting software are also great skills to have.

Updating Your Online Profiles

This may seem like a no-brainer, but I am constantly amazed at the number of LinkedIn profiles that are a year or more behind in terms of a client's career. In some cases, the lack of updates means a job seeker has failed to post a major accomplishment he/she achieved (a significant federal grant obtained, a record-breaking sales quarter for a Fortune 500 company, or publication of an award-winning novel). In other cases, a job seeker's LinkedIn page fails to list their most recent job. You need to keep your online profile(s) updated. From a job seeker's standpoint, you want to keep things updated so when you apply for jobs, a hiring manager can go online and find out about all your latest accomplishments. Do you really want to fail to post that you helped land a company (you were recently laid off from) a business contract that is set to generate millions in revenue? That said, there is another reason to keep your online profile updated, a reason that revolves around actions hiring managers take to screen applicants.

Let's be honest: it's easy to "Google" anyone these days. Consequently, a hiring manager can research you in a matter of seconds to compare your résumé with your online profile (a good method for hiring managers looking to see if a person is lying on her/his résumé). Lack of uniformity between a job seeker's résumé and online profile may suggest a job seeker is trying to hide something. Not the impression you want to make when you are being considered for a position at a new company. Again, updated contact information is something to maintain on your online profile as well as your résumé, but the poor impression an out-of-date online profile provides is the real issue from my experience as a career coach and hiring manager.

Now, what updates should take precedence (on LinkedIn and your physical résumé)? You want to highlight accomplishments and experience that best relate to a job you are applying for. For a résumé, making modifications in this regard is important for every job applied to (in other words, alter each résumé for each job applied to). An online profile like that on LinkedIn is not so easy to keep updated, especially when you are newly out of work and applying for multiple jobs at once. In such an instance, when applying for say four jobs at the same time, which job do you adjust your online profile to suit? Yes, adjust to suit the job you want most, but you still need to make an online profile relevant to the other jobs you are applying to. The nice thing about online profiles is that the "one-page" standard for résumés doesn't really apply. While you don't want to post pages and pages of narrative on LinkedIn, you will have more space for bullet points detailing more accomplishments than a résumé allows. Now… for the bad news.

Hiring managers are looking at the digital footprint of job applicants, which means a hiring manager may look beyond LinkedIn profiles. What you post on Twitter, blogs, YouTube, Facebook, Pinterest, and Instagram could all be examined when a hiring manager is considering your application (right or wrong). Therefore, when updating your online profile, you must examine your entire digital footprint and make adjustments as needed (take down inappropriate photos and delete divisive blog posts/Tweets. True, it's difficult to eradicate posts once they reach the internet, but there are some messes that can be cleaned up. Consider the following steps while preparing your digital footprint for scrutiny:

- **Google yourself.** Use Google and at least two other search engines to see what pops up about yourself. This simple act is a huge eye opener for most people. You will see photos, blog posts, and Tweets from your accounts, as well as other peoples' social media accounts (friends, family, and colleagues). Are you happy with what you see? Would your parents be happy with what shows up (especially within the first three pages of results)? This simple search will let you know how much work you have ahead of you.
- **Delete the negative…if possible.** You will have some ability to control what's online. You can delete blog posts, Tweets, and other online postings (text or photos). Do it whenever possible. Remember, when your posts are "shared" by followers, you lose a lot of control. If something negative shows up on a friend's social media site (a picture of you drunk), contact the friend and ask that the post be deleted. Also, it is at this stage that you should consider blocks on who can view your sites. Your Facebook page, for example, is probably where big-issue posts may show up. Limit who can view your page.
- **Upload the positive.** Post blog entries, Tweets, and other social media entries that reflect the positive accomplishments and activities in your life. Include posts on best-practices within your career field, images of you doing charity work, and inspiring Tweets encouraging others to support causes you are passionate about. Also, those accomplishments you mentioned on your résumé, submit blurbs on those accomplishments

to local newspapers and the alumni offices from your college and high school alma maters. If a local newspaper then posts that information on their website, it becomes a positive for your digital footprint. These positive posts could potentially bury any negative posts that you can't erase.

- **STOP POSTING INAPPROPRIATE MATERIAL!** Blog rants about past employers, highly political rants over controversial issues, and images of you drunk or fighting are not something you should be posting, because they can hurt your chances of getting and keeping a job. For those wanting to remain outspoken advocates for one cause or another (a cause you know deeply divides your community), create an anonymous account on Twitter to use to speak out. Otherwise, you will make it difficult to obtain a new job.
- **Upload solid references.** Whether on LinkedIn or some other platform, upload strong references written by professionals in your field. These references may just pop up quickly in a Google search and make a good impression. Good enough to help a hiring manager overlook negative posts/images.

3

RÉSUMÉ: BASICS FOR SUCCESS

After spending thousands of dollars on a college education, it's remarkable that students usually leave college without any experience in or knowledge of writing a professional résumé. For the record, colleges generally offer free training in writing résumés and cover letters through the college's career center, but students rarely make use of such training. For alumni, they still likely have the ability to get résumé assistance from their college alma mater, though they may be charged a nominal fee to work with the career center's career counselors. That said, below are some basics that I find cover areas that job seekers struggle with the most.

The Structure of a Résumé

In reality, there are multiple viewpoints as to what is the best résumé format. However, if a hundred career specialists were locked in a room and asked to collaborate writing a general résumé, the following would likely be on the final product:

- **Personal Contact information.** Every résumé needs to

provide contact information for the job seeker. As an FYI, I recommend you only include one phone number: the phone number you use as your primary cell or phone number. When looking over candidates and planning to call to schedule interviews, I HATE having to pick through a list of phone numbers, especially when one or more of the listed numbers turns out to be disconnected. That happens a lot.

- **Education.** Whether you are a high school graduate or a college graduate, you need to include a list of your highest educational progress. Important to note: once you start a college career, you no longer need to include your high school information, because it's generally understood you need to graduate high school or successfully complete a GED in order to get into college. As an aside, if you are applying for an entry level job and you know the hiring manager is an alum of your high school, you might want to consider adding your high school information along with your college information. However, even in such rare circumstances, I doubt having your high school information listed will make much of an impact on a hiring manager's decision. For seasoned professionals, it is also worth considering the inclusion of a "Professional Development" section in which you list continuing education units you complete whether as online workshops, conference workshops, or presentations/trainings completed at a job.
- **Professional and Volunteer Experience.** Your résumé obviously needs to include any relevant employment and volunteer history you have. As a new graduate of high school or college, however, you likely have an employment background that includes mostly non-relevant employment, such as working in the service

industry (waiter, cook, cashier, dishwasher, telemarketer, etc.). Hiring managers generally understand this reality so don't be ashamed to include such experience.

- **Technical Proficiencies.** More and more jobs rely on technology to complete even the most rudimentary of tasks. Therefore, it is important to include a list of what programs you have experience with. As an important aside, there are a few programs that are nearly universal in usage, which includes Microsoft Excel, Microsoft Access, and Microsoft Word. Also, given the COVID Pandemic and the increased use of Zoom and similar virtual technologies, it is important to list any such technologies you are proficient in. "Virtual' meetings are likely to remain a popular thing for the near future. Frankly, virtual meetings may become the norm even after the pandemic fades into memory.
- **References.** I remember putting a "References" section on my résumé and writing after it "available upon request." Doing so is a waste of valuable space and time (space on your résumé for more experience and/or accomplishments) and a waste of a hiring manager's time! The latter point refers to the issue that hiring managers don't want to have to ask applicants for additional information such as references; the references should be included in the application materials. Provide a separate document with your résumé that lists your references.

Marks of a Strong Résumé

I am sure most readers are not shocked by the above listing of components of a basic résumé. Now, when gaining experience and after years of working in a career, other sections/components will be likely added: publications, awards, presentations, and continuing education. Yet, for a recent college or high school graduate, those are not likely to be needed or warranted. That said, in addition to these categories, a quality résumé is polished by the following steps:

- **12 point and easy to read font.** Where twenty years ago, Times Roman was the dominant font used, today there are a number of font styles that are acceptable for use on résumés. I for one often use Calibri these days. The important thing is to use a font style that is easy to read. As for size, 12-point font (in Times Roman) is what I consider the guide. So, whether you use 10-, 11-, or 12-point font, it should be close to the 12-point, Times Roman font size. Additionally, do not use cursive fonts such as "Lucida Handwriting" as such fonts can be incredibly hard to decipher for any readers.

Times Roman 12
Garamond 12
Book Antiqua 12
Arial 11
Calibri 11
Courier New 12
Verdana 10

- **Use Résumé Weight Paper.** The 20lb weight paper used in most printers, copiers, and fax machines is meant for general correspondence and record keeping. For résumés (and cover letters), it is preferable if job seekers use a heavier paper. Most office supply stores actually carry "résumé weight" paper, which takes the guess work out of determining which weight of paper is appropriate. In general, it is 24lb weight paper that is preferred for résumés. As a caution, paper weighted heavier than 24lb may jam in printers.

- **Black Ink and a White or Off-white Paper.** I understand the argument of making 'a statement', but rarely do people pull such statements off well when they use résumé paper color choices other than white or similar shades, such as ivory. After years of serving on hiring committees, I've seen a mix of paper hues from dark purple to black paper with silver printing. Many on hiring committees react negatively to such attempts at creativity and individuality. Now, I've noticed official résumé paper sold recently in hues that are light blues, grays, and yellows. For me, this is dangerous ground, because many hiring managers are still set on the need for the classic white or off-white résumé paper with black printing. For me personally, as long as I can read the print, I'll read and consider a résumé based on the applicant's experience and other qualifications. I will say, however, that I have difficulty reading yellow/gold résumé paper because of glare. Furthermore, silver or similarly light-colored ink/print is hard to read, at least it is for me.
- **Print on one side of the page only.** Now, I understand that résumé paper is expensive, and I know that it is thick enough to print on both sides of a sheet without the ink bleeding through to the other side. However, it is more professional looking to only print on ONE SIDE of a sheet of paper. In the event your résumé needs to be two pages in length, use two sheets of résumé paper. As for lighter weighted paper, printing on just one side may bleed through, which is another reason résumé paper is preferable.
- **Page Numbers and Consistent Headings.** If your résumé requires a second page, make certain you

include page numbers on your résumé, as well as a consistent heading. Should a two- or three-page résumé you send get separated (staple falls out, pages are torn apart, etc.), page numbers and the heading will make it easier for a hiring manager to put your résumé pieces together.

- **One Page in Length.** As a recent graduate of college or high school, it is unlikely that you have amassed enough experience and credentials to warrant two or more pages for a résumé. If you feel you have a need to go to a second page, but only have enough material to fill one and a half pages, include a "References" section to fill out the remaining space on the second page (include names and contact information for two to three people who have agreed to serve as references).
- **Submit Unblemished Copies of Résumés.** The final résumé you submit should be a clean copy. The résumé should not be wrinkled, stained, or torn. Why? A hiring manager is not likely to want to touch a résumé that is stained with what appears to be coffee, dirt, or blood. You can't be considered for a position if the hiring manager decides not to touch, let alone read, your résumé.

Proper Headings

I know it's a rather simple and straightforward concept: The heading of a résumé. Yet, you'd be surprised how many recent graduates and even seasoned professionals screw this part up. Yes, your headings need to look clear, sharp, and professional! I feel as if many job seekers focus so much on the rest of a résumé's content that they fail to make a heading that is clear while also looking professional. For example, what do you think of the following as a heading?

Jane Smith

123 Main Street, Somewhere, NY 00000

555-555-555 (home) 555-000-0000 (office)

Iamawesome@email.com

This fictional person's contact information is presented in a format similar to what I encountered multiple times in the past. From a plus side, the individual provided her contact information including home address, phone numbers, and an email. Additionally, this person's information was presented in a single font, which I prefer to see as opposed to one font for the name, a different font for the home address, and then other fonts for phone numbers and email addresses. Now, I understand the idea of standing out, but job seekers (new graduates especially) often overdo résumé creativity. What's worse, some "professional résumé writers" push creative designs that frankly just don't work. I have seen such "professionally made" designs where the attempt at flair was way off the mark. For a basic design that looks professional and sharp looking, I recommend that your résumé heading divert from the above sample in the following ways:

- **Have the heading (name and contact information) centered**. When the heading is off to the left or right side of the page as in the sample above, the job seeker's name becomes minimized. I prefer to see the job seeker's name centered with her or his name a larger font size and bold faced. For example, when using Times Roman font, have the job seeker's name in 16-point font and the contact information in 12-point font.

Jane Smith
123 Main Street, Somewhere, NY 00000
555-555-555 (home) 555-000-0000 (office)
Iamawesome@email.com

- **Use separate lines for the street address and state/zip code**. The sample above can confuse readers a bit, because the address presents a lot of commas. While using an extra line reduces space for experience, certifications, and other information, it makes it easier for hiring managers to see the home address.

Jane Smith
123 Main Street
Somewhere, NY 00000
555-555-555 (home) 555-000-0000 (office)
Iamawesome@email.com

- **List one phone number**. Hiring managers do not want to have to guess which number is the best way to reach you. With most individuals owning cell phones these days, most job seekers should have a mobile number to provide that they can keep with them at all times. Additionally, the sample provided listed a home AND an office number, which is a no-no. Providing a hiring manager with your current work phone number is unprofessional to say the least. Think about it! You are essentially telling potential employers that you will answer their calls while working at another job. The hiring manager may think that in the future, if hired, you will think nothing of answering personal calls while on the job. Not an impression you want to make. Provide a personal cell phone or home phone number, one or the other. Furthermore, make certain the voice message system connected with that phone includes a professional message. For example, "I'm not here just leave a message" or "You know what to do at the sound of the beep" are not appropriate messages. Also, voice mail that includes music or has a message that tricks a caller into thinking they reached you only to hear you laugh and say "fooled you" is unprofessional. At best, a hiring manager will think you juvenile should your cell phone voice mail sound like any of the above. At worst, the hiring manager will hang up and shred your résumé. That said, the following heading is a preferred way to go.

Jane Smith
123 Main Street
Somewhere, NY 00000
555-555-555
Iamawesome@email.com

- **Use a professional email**. The email in the above samples is rather tame compared to many emails I've seen listed on résumés, which includes résumés for seasoned professionals who are experienced managers. Everything from usernames describing a job seeker's body parts to references to their favorite superhero have come across my desk. I'm willing to look beyond such indiscretions, while many, if not most, hiring managers are not. For safety's sake, avoid anything along the lines of the following: bootilicious@email.com, hotass@email.com, punk100@email.com, thegreatone@email.com, ironman300@email.com or mrawesome@email.com. Leave such email addresses for contacting friends. For professional contacts, especially for your résumé, keep it basic: your first initial and last name. You may also need to include a number after the name, because your name might be similar to others but that at least gives you an email that is less likely to offend a sensitive hiring manager.

Jane Smith
123 Main Street
Somewhere, NY 00000
555-555-555
JSmith44@email.com

This heading format may seem a bit boring, but it is clear and to the point. The other nice thing about this heading format, at least for those recent graduates with little experience and in need of filler for their résumé, is that it can fill unused space. When space becomes an issue after a few years of employment, try some of the following alternates to add a bit of professional spice to your résumé.

Jane Smith
123 Main Street • Somewhere, NY 00000
555.555.5555 • jsmith44@email.com

123 Main Street • Somewhere, NY 00000
555.555.5555 • jsmith44@email.com
Jane Smith

Jane Smith

---

123 Smith Street | Somewhere, NY 00000 | 555.555.5555 | jsmith44@email.com

4

JOB SEARCH THROUGH YOUR NETWORK

When I was laid off in 2003, I was embarrassed and felt I had failed myself, my family, and my college advisors. Frankly, the experience was gut-wrenching, and I delayed speaking with my network because of the shame I felt. That was a mistake, because it delayed my network's assistance in helping me find jobs to apply for. I have long been an advocate of college students starting early to build connections to help find employment opportunities, and yet, here I was avoiding my network altogether because of shame and embarrassment. I am writing this chapter as if I could go back to 2003 and give myself a good heart-to-heart chat. Here's what I would tell myself if I could travel back through time:

- **You lost your job… Get over it, because a lot of people in your network have lost jobs, too!** After I let people know I lost my job, a number of them told me about jobs they were laid off or outright fired from. Those conversations made me feel better and realize the layoff was just part of life's journey. I even learned of others who had lost jobs right before or after they were married as was my situation. You are in no way alone in your circumstances. One job loss does not define us or our legacy. Pick yourself up, dust yourself off, and seek better opportunities.

- **Notify your network immediately of any job loss!** Delaying even a week before notifying your network of family, friends, and colleagues of a job loss means one full week of their not being able to help you find a new job. That could mean a hundred job openings that you will never be able to apply for, simply because you were too embarrassed to let people know you were fired or laid off. I learned that during the delay in telling my network of my layoff, there were multiple job openings that I was well qualified for, but I had missed the application deadline. Additionally, there were employment opportunities I would have been immediately hired for had my network connection at the company known I was looking for a job. Any delay can hurt your job search and limit your opportunities.
- **Ask individuals in your network to keep an eye out for job openings.** Just notifying your network of a job loss is not enough. People in your network may assume you already have a job lined up and not let you know of job openings at their companies unless you directly ask them to keep a look out for job openings that fit your abilities, experience, and education.
- **Ask your network about any volunteer opportunities within their respective companies.** Again, while unemployed, it is critical to get any experience that would increase your skill sets and provide experience to hopefully overshadow the job lost. Volunteering in a capacity related to your career can do this. For example, for accountants, ask to volunteer at a bank or credit union in a teller or accountant position. Not only would

such experience be relevant when applying for a new job, such volunteer experience could lead to your being considered for future job openings at that company. As for relevant volunteer experiences to consider, speak with those in your network who are professionals in the same industry for guidance to suitable volunteer opportunities.

- **Ask individuals in your network (who are specialists in the same career as you) to post recommendations for you on LinkedIn and other online sites.** In addition to having your network prepare written recommendations for when you apply for jobs, seek to have three to five individuals post recommendations on your LinkedIn page to further develop your digital profile/footprint in a positive light.
- **Thank your network along the way.** Whether it's taking a friend or colleague out for coffee or simply sending them a periodic email to say you appreciate their assistance, thank you notes and gestures are critical, because it helps keep you in their thoughts and, more importantly, it's the right thing to do.

5

USING ONLINE SEARCH ENGINES

In this new digital age, I am amazed at the number of people whose job search is limited to looking at job listings in local, regional, and national newspapers. The World Wide Web offers a vast range of outlets for searching for jobs. In fact, focusing on internet-based search engines is often all that is needed to locate good jobs. For crying out loud, you can usually access the job ads for newspapers on their own websites, saving you the time to pick up a physical newspaper (looking online also will usually save you the cost of the newspaper). Now, before listing major search engines to consider, I would like to list a warning. Online sites like 'Craigslist' may offer job opportunities that fit your needs perfectly. However, there have been instances where opportunities turned into nightmares for people who answered online ads. Before setting up a meeting with anyone through a website ad, make certain the meeting is in a public place and that someone knows you are going to the meeting. Better yet, ask someone to drive you. Be safe. As for job search engines, consider the following:

- Monster.com

- Careerbuilder.com
- Indeed.com
- LinkedIn.com
- USAJobs.gov
- Glassdoor.com
- Ziprecruiter.com
- Justjobs.com
- Simplyhired.com
- Juju.com
- Hound.com
- Ihire.com
- Theladders.com
- Recruiter.com
- Jobspider.com
- Snagajob.com

The importance of online search engines is not just that they provide continually updated listings of jobs. Such websites usually also provide articles by career counselors like myself that cover a range of topics, including how to write a cover letter, what are the most common job interview questions, writing a professional résumé that gets noticed, and unique places to find job listings. Many of these sites also allow you to post your résumé, which is another way to connect with potential employers. I recommend you speak with those within your network (particularly those who work in your field) to see which search engines they have had the most luck with.

Unique Places to Look for Jobs

In addition to job search engines, I recommend job seekers to visit company websites directly, because many companies seek to save the cost of job ads by just posting job openings on their own website. Speak with professionals in your field about companies you should consider employment with and then see if the company has listed any jobs. If no jobs are listed, consider sending a cover letter and résumé, asking the company to keep you in mind should any job opportunities become available that match your skills and experience. Lastly, check local newspapers, community newsletters, and even church bulletins for job ads. A lot of local businesses utilize such outlets as their primary source of advertising, because these outlets are relatively inexpensive.

6

EMPLOYMENT AT COLLEGES AND NON-PROFITS

The world is filled with colleges, universities, hospitals, clinics, museums, zoos, community centers, homeless shelters, and an assortment of other non-profit organizations that offer educational, healthcare, and other support to local, regional, and national communities. Now, for the unemployed, such institutions may provide counselors to assist individuals with job searches. However, that is not why I put in this chapter. Especially in the instances of colleges and universities, these institutions have become cities in and of themselves. As with any traditional city, these institutions need a great variety of employees, which includes very specialized professionals (accountants, attorneys, architects, bakers, chefs, computer programmers, counselors, electricians, engineers, librarians, media consultants, nurses, paralegals, physicians, secretaries, and teachers). These institutions also often need general laborers to work as administrative assistants, cooks, customer service representatives, groundskeepers, janitors, maintenance workers, painters, and sales personnel. Admittedly, such positions may pay less in salary/per hour than similar positions in private companies (although benefits such as retirement funds and health insurance can often be good at non-profits). Also, specialist positions at non-profit institutions are often funded by grants and set to last only one or a few years (as was the case of my position I was laid off from). The beauty in this is that people who work in non-profits often stay for only a limited time — usually just long enough to find a full-time job with a private company. Therefore, employee turnover may be high, which ultimately means jobs can open up quickly at such institutions. Without a job, work at a non-profit could help you gain good experience and provide better financial support than unemployment insurance, so take a look at non-profits.

7

ADDRESSING BEING FIRED OR LAID OFF IN AN INTERVIEW

It is hard to address any questions regarding why you were laid off or fired. Job seekers are afraid to answer the question while hiring managers and hiring committees are petrified to ask it. That said, it is better to prepare for the question than to hope it won't be asked when you are in a job interview. For those laid off due to cutbacks or a position's grant funding ending, it's relatively straightforward with regards to answering the question. Simply inform the hiring manager or committee that you were hired for a set period of time and you completed the project(s) you were assigned. It would be a good idea to compliment the company and supervisor you worked for, adding that you learned a great deal from the experience that you could bring to the job you are applying to (i.e., mention skill sets you learned/utilized at your last job that would be relevant and beneficial to the job you are applying for). You should also mention training you received at the job you were laid off from and any instances where you trained others on staff. Lastly, make certain you include at least one reference from the company you were laid off from. In the interview, mention what that reference would say about your character and work ethic. I was quite fortunate that both my boss and immediate supervisor wrote amazing recommendations for me (thank you Bill and Walt). Now for the hard one: **how to handle questions about why you were fired**.

How to Address Being Fired in a Job Interview

It's not an easy thing to discuss, having been fired. Yet, in a job interview, there may be no way to get around it. Hiring managers and hiring committees often ask why an individual left a previous job. When it comes to a firing, I think there will always be hiring managers who are hesitant to hire a job seeker who was recently fired. Many try to leave it at saying something along the lines of "I quit the job because it just wasn't a good fit anymore." Trying to lie yourself out of it is not only dishonest, but it also will backfire in a big way if anyone on the hiring committee knows you were fired. Considering you will never know what inside information a hiring manager or committee has on you, I think it is good practice to always be truthful.

The question is, what details are important to discuss regarding your being fired? To guide you through this would-be minefield, consider the following advice:

- **Don't be critical of the employer who fired you.** As I said, you will never know what insider information they have acquired about you. Someone interviewing you may be best friends with the person that fired you. Even if the interviewer(s) don't know the person who fired you, they will likely be hesitant to hire you if you take time to trash the reputation, policies, and abilities of a previous employer. Why? Because they may worry about how you will talk about them IF you are hired. Many of us have experience in overly critical people who seem to gossip or talk negatively about people not in the room. Most of us avoid such individuals, because we are fearful they will damage the unity amongst colleagues. Keep things simple and polite. Simply say that the last job and/or employer taught you a lot about the industry, but mention it just wasn't the best fit. Here is the time to also show off your research skills; do research on the company interviewing you and mention at this point that you feel their goals match well with your skills, goals, and accomplishments.

- **Mention your accomplishments at your previous job.** It usually helps in an interview if you can mention statistics that make you look good. If you were fired from a job, mentioning that you increased sales by 20% or that you helped develop a new ad campaign would help offset being fired. In fact, someone with a good number of accomplishments from a job they were fired from could significantly improve their chances of getting a job, especially if their accomplishments are aligned with the new job's duties. Such accomplishments will often have a hiring manager overlooking your having been fired.
- **Provide a reference from your last job who will speak to your strengths and accomplishments.** Even being able to note one person from the company that fired you, someone who can vouch for your abilities, could make all the difference: "If you speak with Jane Smith, Director of Communications, she will tell you that I was solely responsible for landing a $10,000 grant to fund our network upgrade."
- **Volunteer at a non-profit organization in a capacity to increase skills while simultaneously building up new references.** Museums, colleges, high schools, libraries, and multiple other community organizations are in dire need of volunteers to help with grant writing,

data processing, mentoring, records management, advertising, social media outreach, mentoring, and countless other tasks, which will undoubtedly be relevant to your skills and the jobs you are seeking. Even volunteering five hours per week could build up experience that a hiring manager will place more weight on than your previous firing.

- **Find freelancing opportunities to build skills, acquire field contacts, and lessen the impact of a recent firing.** Freelancing or working as a subcontractor in capacities requiring your talents could help you build up skill sets, experience, and references that could make it easier to downplay a firing. What's more, freelancing could provide a new revenue source and even lead to your finding a new career path (i.e., starting your own business). You should check to see how freelancing will impact any unemployment benefits you have before accepting any freelance work.

I wish there was an easy way to just erase a firing from a person's employment history, but we both know that isn't reality. Armed with the aforementioned advice, however, you can help lessen the impact of getting fired. As a final bit of advice, as you prepare for interviews, ask and answer for yourself the following questions with regards to the job you were fired from:

1. Was I entrusted to train new employees at the last job?
2. Was I a part of major decisions with regards to the company's future goals/plans?
3. Was I part of any hiring committees that interviewed for upper management positions at the company?
4. Did I institute any policies or programs that are still in use at the company today?

5. Did I serve as a consultant for the company in any capacity?
6. Did I enhance any programs, which ultimately led to increased sales and/or production?
7. Did any of my work obtain the attention of media in a positive light?
8. Was I selected by any manager to represent the company at a conference or business-related function?
9. Did I present at training seminars or conferences during which I discussed the company's accomplishments?
10. Did I obtain a patent for work I created/completed at my last job?
11. Did I create any websites, newsletters, or other materials with which the company was able to update the public, media, investors, and employees?
12. Am I still being asked to come back and train employees in any capacity at the job I was fired from?
13. Did I spearhead any technological or methodological advances at my previous employer?

All of these accomplishments indicate an individual's opinion and skills were important to a past employer, and anyone interviewing you will likely be more inclined to hire you knowing these facts. Why? Because such accomplishments indicate you were valued by someone at your last job.

8

FINAL TIPS FOR SUCCESS

There you have it — my advisement for when you have lost your job and need to find a new job. Let me say that I hate to see anyone lose a job, especially when they have a family to support. I hope you find the advice here helpful to you. Please remember that I also have advice posted on my free blog (https://professionwise.com/). I also am happy to answer any questions you may have via my Twitter feed (@Neil_ODonnell). In closing, let me simply say that I wish you the best as you venture forward, and I hope that you quickly find a job that is more satisfying and better paying than the one you lost. Whatever led to the job loss, you now have a fresh start and can either continue on with your chosen profession or go off on a new career journey. You have more choices than you may realize. Simply reach out to career professionals for guidance like fellow specialists with the Professional Association of Résumé Writers and Career Coaches (http://www.parw.com/) and ask for help.

Dear reader,

We hope you enjoyed reading *A Job Search After Job Loss*. Please take a moment to leave a review, even if it's a short one. Your opinion is important to us.

Discover more books by Neil O'Donnell at https://www.nextchapter.pub/authors/neil-odonnell

Want to know when one of our books is free or discounted? Join the newsletter at http://eepurl.com/bqqB3H

Best regards,
Neil O'Donnell and the Next Chapter Team

Job Search After Job Loss
ISBN: 978-4-86750-337-9

Published by
Next Chapter
1-60-20 Minami-Otsuka
170-0005 Toshima-Ku, Tokyo
+818035793528

4th June 2021

www.ingramcontent.com/pod-product-compliance
Lightning Source LLC
LaVergne TN
LVHW041517190726
843491LV00009B/2759

* 9 7 8 4 8 6 7 5 0 3 3 7 9 *